CW00801526

SKY HIGH
ISLE OF WIGHT

PHOTOGRAPHY BY JASON HAWKES

First published in Great Britain in 2009

Photographs © 2009 Jason Hawkes

British Library Cataloguing-in-Publication Data
A CIP record for this title is available from the British Library

ISBN 978 1 906887 54 4

PiXZ Books
Halsgrove House, Ryelands Industrial Estate,
Bagley Road, Wellington, Somerset TA21 9PZ
Tel: 01823 653777
Fax: 01823 216796
email: sales@halsgrove.com

An imprint of Halstar Ltd, part of the Halsgrove group of companies
Information on all Halsgrove titles is available at: www.halsgrove.com

Printed and bound by Grafiche Flaminia, Italy

Introduction

The Isle of Wight was once an independent kingdom and, while it no longer enjoys this status, it does still retain an atmosphere of separateness – an island unto itself. The superb aerial photographs in this book provide a fascinating overview of this historic island community, which these days provides a distinctive place to live for thousands, and for many more a place to enjoy leisure pursuits including watersports of all kinds, birdwatching, or simply walking the many island footpaths.

Jason Hawkes is one of the country's best-known photographers specialising in aerial photography. The photographs in this book are selected to provide the reader with a bird's-eye view of a variety of landscapes and settlements, with historic sites included.

For visitors to the Isle of Wight, or as reminder to locals of what is best about their home, this little book is an ideal memento.

The River Yar, Yarmouth on the right and the mainland distant.

Yarmouth looking west.

The Isle of Wight Ferry terminal, Yarmouth.

The centre of Yarmouth.

The harbour and lifeboat station, Yarmouth.

Looking across Totland Bay to Totland and a distant Freshwater.

Right: Hatherwood Point and Alum Bay.

Totland, where Church Hill meets York Road.

Fort Redoubt, Freshwater Bay.

Right: Spectacular view of The Needles and the lighthouse.

Above and left: The Needles light.

Looking along the length of the island from above Hatherwood Point.

The view from above the old Coastguard Station and the old battery, Alum Bay left.

The chalk cliff known as Main Bench runs back from Scratchell's Bay.

Freshwater Bay.

Right: A wonderful view above Freshwater Bay towards The Needles, Afton on the right.

The picturesque hamlet of Brook.

Left: An almost abstract picture of cliffs and caves near Freshwater Bay.

Brightstone.

The centre of Brightstone.

Above Brightstone looking out towards The Needles.

The view eastward, Brightstone and Moortown right, with Shorwell mid distant.

Left: The opposite view: inland of Brightstone looking west, with Calbourne distant.

Above and right: Spectacular views eastwards towards St Catherine's Point.

Looking inland from
Brightstone Bay.

Whale Chine, below Pyle.

Left: Shepherd's Chine and the Holiday Centre near Little Atherfield.

The village and church at Chale.

Open country above Chale on St Catherine's Down.

The view south-east above Chale, looking towards St Catherine's Point.

31

Dramatic cliffs at Blackgang with
St Catherine's Hill beyond.

St Catherine's lighthouse at Niton Undercliff.

Looking into the centre of Niton.

The view south over Niton.

The delightfully rural Niton, source of the River Yar.

St Catherine's lighthouse, built in 1840.

Between Niton and Ventnor. The Victorian period saw
many such grand residences being built on the island.

Left: Reeth Bay.

Homes and a holiday park along Undercliff Drive near Niton.

Steephill Cove, west of Ventnor.

The area around St Albans Gardens, Ventnor.

Ventnor Marina.

Left: The western end of the Esplanade, Ventnor.

Housing, near Wheelers Bay Road, Ventnor.

Left: Wheelers Bay.

Sandown and its famous pier.

Left: A superb photograph of Shanklin looking towards Sandown.

47

Culver Down and Whitecliff Bay.

Right: Whitecliff Bay.

The view across the Foreland to Bembridge.

Right: The lifeboat station Bembridge.

East Ryde Sands and North Walk, Ryde.

Looking along the pier at Ryde.

The view south-east over Ryde, the English Channel far distant.

The ferry terminal at Fishbourne.

Sleepy Havenstreet Station on the Isle of Wight Steam Railway.

Osborne House was built c.1850 as Queen Victoria's and Prince Albert's summer residence in East Cowes.

The Prince Consort was largely responsible for the design of the gardens.

Norris Castle, East Cowes, was built in 1790.

Looking from Cowes over to East Cowes.

Right: The view from the Esplanade looking upriver at Cowes.

Cowes is a very busy ferry terminal. One of the famous Red Funnel Line's vessels is seen here.

Another view over Cowes and the River Medina.

The River Medina enters the heart of Newport.

Looking over South Street, Newport.

Right: The aftermath of the Isle of Wight Festival, Newport.

Looking over Newport.